T
7/20/05

D0753232

729.095
B64

ARCHITECTURE & DESIGN LIBRARY

INDIA STYLE

Fashion Institute of Design & Merchandising
Resource & Research Center
55 Stockton St., 5th Floor
San Francisco, CA 94108-5805

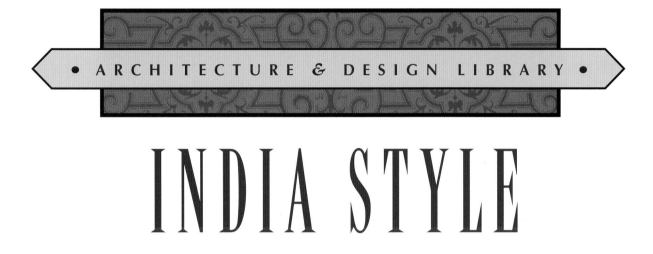

ARCHITECTURE & DESIGN LIBRARY

INDIA STYLE

Alexandra Bonfante-Warren

FRIEDMAN/FAIRFAX

PUBLISHERS

A FRIEDMAN/FAIRFAX BOOK

© 2001 Michael Friedman Publishing Group, Inc.

Please visit our website: www.metrobooks.com

All rights reserved. No part of this publication may be reproduced, stored in a retrieval system, or transmitted, in any form or by any means, electronic, mechanical, photocopying, recording, or otherwise, without prior written permission from the publisher.

Library of Congress Cataloging-in-Publication Data

Bonfante-Warren, Alexandra.
    India style / Alexandra Bonfante-Warren.
      p. cm. -- (Architecture and design library)
    Includes bibliographical references and index.
    ISBN 1-58663-118-7
     1. Interior decoration—Indic influences. 2. Color in interior decoration. 3. Decoration and ornament, Architectural—India. I. Title. II. Series.

NK2115.5.E84 B66 2001
729'.0954--dc21

                                  00-066251

Editor: Hallie Einhorn
Art Director: Jeff Batzli
Designer: Dan Duce Lish
Photography Editor: Kate Perry
Production Manager: Rosy Ngo

Color separations by Colourscan Overseas Co Pte. Ltd
Printed in Hong Kong by Midas Printing Limited

1 3 5 7 9 10 8 6 4 2

Distributed by Sterling Publishing Company, Inc.
387 Park Avenue South
New York, NY 10016
Distributed in Canada by Sterling Publishing
Canadian Manda Group
One Atlantic Avenue, Suite 105
Toronto, Ontario, Canada M6K 3E7
Distributed in Australia by
Capricorn Link (Australia) Pty Ltd.
P.O. Box 6651
Baulkham Hills, Business Centre, NSW 2153, Australia

To Bosa and Linda—and to seeing the wide world.

C o n t e n t s

INTRODUCTION

Warm, enveloping scents of cumin, cardamom, ginger, and turmeric; the reflective twang of sitar and the furious tap of tabla; brilliant rainbow-hued silks so fine they pass through a bride's wedding ring—these are just a few of India's infinite treasures. Only half the area of the United States, India has close to a billion inhabitants, speaking fourteen official languages and hundreds of dialects, and practicing eight major religions as well as countless variants. Even the geography features a tremendous amount of diversity, from the Himalayas—boasting the world's highest peaks—to the fertile plains of the great Ganges River and the deserted, Edenic beaches. The nation's history is no less rich, comprising thousands of years of migrations and invasions, all of which have influenced numerous aspects of Indian culture, including architecture and design.

The religious life of India is often intense, expressed in the sinuous sculptures of Hindu gods and goddesses, as well as in the rhythmic tracery of the arches and domes of Islamic architecture. Spiritual influences are apparent in residences throughout the country, from the mansions of movie stars in Bombay, or "Bollywood," to the mud houses of shepherds in rural areas. In the cities, processions wind through busy streets, celebrating weddings, funerals, and revered deities.

To gain a better appreciation of Indian architecture and design, it helps to become acquainted with the history of India's religious and cultural influences. As early as 3500 B.C.E., an urban society developed in the valley of the Indus River, and it was the gods of these Dravidians who ultimately became transformed into Hindu deities. During the following millennium, invading Aryans from Afghanistan and central Asia settled in the plains of the Ganges River. While the Dravidian cults were predecessors of Hinduism, it was the Vedas, the sacred scriptures of the Aryans, that gave shape to this religion, which is currently practiced by more than 700 million people in India. In turn, Hinduism developed a unified system of colors, elements, and divine forces that influences every part of the lives of the faithful—including home construction and design.

OPPOSITE: *In this comfortable living room, stenciled designs highlight a wide scalloped arch in true Indian style, while a graceful textile treatment, known as a* toran, *hangs at the top of a window for an air of distinction. Formal white makes every accent count, from the stripes on the pillows to the cherished objects on the coffee table.*

Between the sixth and fourth centuries B.C.E., two invasions from the north left their mark. The first was the incursion by the Persian king Darius, known as "The Great," who annexed the Punjab and Sind in the northwest. The second invasion—that of Alexander the Great—is better known, though it failed. In 326 B.C.E., the Macedonian king marched into northern India after conquering Persia; but upon reaching the Beas River, his exhausted troops refused to go any farther. Tradition has it that the thirty-year-old leader, who had three more years to live, wept because he had no more worlds to conquer.

Although the invasion did not succeed, it did leave a lasting impact upon eastern India. After Alexander and his soldiers withdrew, there arose the singular Gandharan subculture, wedding Greek artistic tenets with the religious tenets of Buddhism, a new religion that had grown out of Hinduism. Over the following centuries, Buddhism and Hinduism succeeded each other as the predominant belief system in India, with Hinduism prevailing. Ultimately, the Hindus immortalized the Buddha as an avatar of their god Vishnu, the sustainer.

The religious and artistic diversity does not stop with Hinduism and Buddhism. Around the year 1000 C.E., Muslim warriors began a series of invasions that would, over the next four centuries, establish Islam in northern India and lay the foundations for an empire that would cover most of the subcontinent. One of the most visible legacies of the Muslims is their architecture, with its variety of ornate arches that grace constructions of yesteryear and today. The iconoclastic Muslims, however, destroyed much of the native art that they found, from Buddhist cave paintings celebrating creation to the magnificent Jain temples.

In 1526, Babur, a descendant of Genghis Khan, established the Mughal dynasty in India. These powerful emperors, strongly influenced by the courtly, poetic Persian style, were great patrons of the arts, and their tradition, manifest chiefly in architecture and painting, would endure until the British occupation in the nineteenth century.

The most famous Indian icon of all, the Taj Mahal, was built by a Mughal emperor, Shah Jahan.

In the south, the Hindu states allied against the Muslims, creating, by the fourteenth century, a powerful empire that was to become one of the wealthiest in India's history. The fertile coastal plains supplied an unmatched agricultural bounty, and the world's goods poured in through the famous trade routes that had been forged centuries earlier.

It was in the first century C.E. that Chinese silk traders under the Han dynasty began to take their merchandise into central Asia. As the Roman Empire expanded eastward, a trading route took shape. With its start in the third century C.E., the Silk Road would last for some thirteen hundred years, bringing Chinese silks through northwest India and bearing away precious stones and such precious metals as gold and silver. Indian textile workers developed techniques for adorning the highly valued silks—which inspired the growth of India's own luxury silk industry—as well as for decorating the fine cottons that are still a major export. The handiwork of Indian craftspeople became widely prized.

During the fifteenth and sixteenth centuries—the Age of Exploration—Portuguese navigators rounded Africa's Cape of Good Hope and headed to India for the spices worth more than gold. The Dutch were not far behind, establishing trading posts in 1595. Christian missionaries followed in the traders' wake, adding yet another layer to the religious fabric of India. And Jews exiled from their homes in Portugal and Spain had arrived during the late fifteenth

OPPOSITE: *Shah Jahan built the Taj Mahal as a memorial to Mumtaz Mahal, his favorite wife. Construction began in 1632, the year after her death, and proceeded for approximately seventeen years.*

century. Trade, emigration, and proselytism gave rise to cities, such as lively Cochin in the southwest. Once on the spice route, this city still boasts synagogues and cathedrals among its marketplaces and other houses of worship.

The British came to India to partake in the spice trade, officially establishing their East India Company on December 31, 1600. In some homes, the European influence radically changed Indian social customs. No longer did everyone sit on the floor. Instead, tables and chairs took up permanent residence in rooms whose functions had previously been flexible. The British occupation left a variety of legacies, from its bureaucratic structure to the use of Victorian gingerbread flourishes on wooden houses.

Meanwhile, in western Europe, Indian cottons arrived as treasured fabrics. In the 1600s, so great was the demand in France that an illegal business in forged Indian cottons thrived—especially in the southern region. Today, these printed designs, originally imitations of Indian imports, are considered typical of Provence.

During the twentieth century, Mahatma Gandhi, who led the Indian independence movement that culminated in 1947 with India becoming a sovereign state, encouraged Indians to continue producing their world-renowned textiles for their economic benefit. Could the Mahatma have predicted an unexpected surge in demand from an unlikely source? In the 1950s, a small and loosely connected—but influential—group of poets and other artists in the United States, disturbed perhaps by the ravenous postwar consumerism, looked to the spirituality of Asia, especially Buddhism, as an alternative. Many traveled to India to study with spiritual masters—a trend that became a flood during the prosperous 1960s. Bells jangled on wrists and ankles, and Indian prints adorned beds, couches, chairs, cushions, walls, windows, and tables, bringing a sensual elegance to Western interiors.

Today, India's textiles, furnishings, and colorful accents are once again enjoying a tremendous amount of appreciation in Western fashion and home design. Just a breath of Indian style can give a home an exotic and even magical feel. A length of sari silk edged in majestic gold and fluttering in front of a window will delicately tint surrounding walls. An airy tent of mosquito netting brings a languorous hint of tropical India into a cool bedroom. On a tabletop, a brass bowl filled with dried petals adds a gracious touch.

Thanks to India's diverse cultural and religious makeup, Indian style has a flexibility that always leaves room for individual flair. The most illuminating example of this concept lies, perhaps, in curry— India's best-known food. There is no single curry, because each cook prepares an individual mix, to taste. Similarly, a *masala*—an idiosyncratic mixture of spices—varies from cook to cook, and from season to season, depending upon what is good or just available in the market.

Look around, consider the feel you wish your rooms to have, explore the vast variety of Indian architectural elements, fabrics, accents, and colors, and prepare your own unique masala of Indian style.

OPPOSITE: *These scalloped arches and the picturesque landscape they frame could be found nowhere but in India. The fusion of cultures over the course of millennia has created a complex yet accessible tradition in the decorative arts.*

OPPOSITE: *A stately pavilion lends a regal quality to outdoor dining. Foliated arches in quick succession allow breezes to waft through while presenting spectacular views of Delhi. The city is actually the seventh urban incarnation on the site, restored in the seventeenth century by the legendary Mughal emperor Shah Jahan.*

ABOVE: *Readily adaptable, Indian craftsmanship can find itself perfectly at home in all sorts of settings. This carved wood door and surround from India, for instance, takes up residence at a villa in Mexico. Thanks to the natural beauty of the wood, this architectural element fits in effortlessly with the surroundings. An exuberant cascade of bougainvillea, the brilliant flower of the tropics, provides a fitting and lively accent.*

CHAPTER ONE

ARCHITECTURAL DETAILS

The range of architectural styles in India is great, reflecting differences in climate, cultural background, and lifestyle. The spectrum includes not only the royal *mahals*, or palaces, of Rajasthan and the grand *havelis*, or mansions, of Jaipur, but also the houseboats of Kashmir, the hand-built mud dwellings of the Thar Desert, and the Art Deco, modernist, and postmodern showcases of Delhi.

In India's more extreme climates—such as the Himalayas, which experience fierce and frigid winters, and the desert, which is subject to relentless heat—homes are usually built with thick walls and small windows. (The classic domes of India, regal appurtenances of the great tombs and palaces, also serve to receive the heat rising from the lower part of a room.) Elsewhere, however, most buildings are designed so as to encourage the circulation of air between outdoors and in, as well as from room to room. This strategy not only provides comfort, but adheres to the rules of *Vastu Shastra*. The Indian equivalent of *feng shui*, and perhaps an inspiration for the later Pythagorean systems of Greece, Vastu Shastra lays out principles for building and decorating various constructions, including homes. According to this ancient science, structures should, for instance, have square rooms and an even number of windows. Some interpretations speak of the familiar four elements—earth, air or wind, fire, and water; according to others, there is a fifth element—space, or sky.

A proper circulation of air assures an analogous current of well-being, and Indian design offers a number of ways to keep the sun's heat out while inviting in air and light. One of the most decorative of these solutions is the *jali*, a pierced panel inspired by the Muslim *moushrabiya*. This feature was originally designed to allow the women of the house to look out a window without themselves being seen. Today, the jali can contribute an Indian flair to any home, whether gracing a window or enlivening a wall panel with texture and pattern.

OPPOSITE: *During the nineteenth century, British visitors to India wrote that the architecture and interiors they saw demonstrated an exquisite balance between empty and full. Here, intricately detailed mullions paired with large, smooth panes of glass express this sense of equilibrium. Inside, a vast wall is punctuated by a decorative niche, which is, in turn, highlighted with a stenciled design.*

Traditional Indian architecture never fails to adorn a doorway. The arrival of family and guests is always an occasion, and the movement from outdoors to indoors, a rite of passage. The importance of this transition and the accompanying sense of hospitality are reflected in the decorative attention that doorways receive. Some are enhanced with color, others with personal variations on timeless geometric motifs; but regardless of the specific type of embellishment, the sentiment expressed is one of welcome.

Reflective surfaces are also characteristic of homes in India. The popularity of such surfaces arises, perhaps, from necessity; the price of a cool interior may be dimness, mitigated by mirrored surfaces. Prized for its glossy quality, *airaish*, a polished eggshell stucco, is often used for flooring and in some cases for walls. While its luster is somewhat more subtle than that of marble, airaish offers the benefit of being equally low-maintenance.

Indian decoration is often a sophisticated combination of profusion and emptiness, and interiors are no exception. One of the first qualities that will strike a visitor upon entering an Indian residence—even a modest home in a crowded city—is a powerful sensation of space. Homes exhibit a communal quality, as evidenced by the *baithak*, a common or reception room that serves as living area, dining area, and on occasion, guest room. In small houses, the few rooms that make up the dwelling will flow easily into one another, or into a courtyard or garden, thereby enhancing the feeling of space. The transition can be marked by something as humble as a simple wood lintel or as grand as an elaborate arch. From plain plaster spans that are elegant in their understatement to ornate cusped affairs surmounting pillars in the Muslim fashion, the possibilities are numerous. Carved wood or fretwork panels can also delineate a boundary. Painted, a simple fretwork panel can act as a room divider that paradoxically appears to double the space while lending a touch of tradition and an air of importance to the surroundings.

The spacious quality of Indian rooms can set off a selective profusion of decorative details, which may appear anywhere and everywhere. Such ornamentation may include ceilings of elaborately carved wood or simple frescoed designs, stenciled motifs highlighting architectural features, and built-in niches housing cherished objects. Walls, both inside and out, can sport intricately carved panels in timeless geometric arrangements or spontaneous tributes to nature.

If an Englishman's home is his castle, the Indian home is a temple of hospitality that nurtures the spiritual and physical health of family and friends.

OPPOSITE: *Neemrana Fort Palace serves a more peaceful purpose these days—as a hotel. Welcoming guests with a grand yet gracious statement, this entrance features a Tudor arch framed by a classic scalloped arch. Similar shapes appear in the galleries as well as in the windows.*

ABOVE: *Seemingly floating on water, Udaipur's Lake Palace Hotel was originally built by Maharana Jagat Singh II in 1754 as a royal summer palace. The structure is a mesmerizing confection of pristine white domes and arched windows. Udaipur, known as the City of Sunrise, is home to a plethora of lakeside havelis, palaces, and temples.*

ABOVE, LEFT: *The shape of this arch—which echoes the silhouette of the doorway it frames—creates the impression of parted curtains. As a result, the diminutive perch takes on a theatrical demeanor.*

ABOVE, RIGHT: *A drift of furious pink bougainvillea, a tiny jali highlighted in yellow, and a stylized leaf motif just below the window are enough to stamp this vignette with Indian style. It is easy to imagine the pattern of rich sunlight cast indoors through the jali's traditional design.*

OPPOSITE: *Bada Bagh's five-hundred-year-old domes and sophisticated combination of architectural details honor the kings buried there. The tombs are located near Jaisalmer, the capital of Rajasthan, in the sandy stretches of the Thar Desert.*

ABOVE: *In the arid region of northern Gujarat, the organic lines and decorations of mud architecture prevail. Women execute most of the ornamentation. Here what appears to be a stenciled design is actually an improvised pattern created by pressing leaves into a mud wall.*

RIGHT: *Tipu Sultan of Mysore, who died in 1799, was one of the last rulers in southern India before the British presence became dominant. His summer palace was adorned with carved and painted motifs such as this, intended to inspire thoughts of paradise.*

RIGHT, TOP: *This intricately designed marble panel is part of the Taj Mahal. The fineness of the detailing—from the gentle bend of the stems to the precise ridges in the leaves—seems at once humble and extravagant.*

RIGHT, BOTTOM: *The eight-pointed star, made up of two superimposed squares, is a typical Islamic design element, as is the play of geometric shapes. These, combined with abstract floral patterns, express the aristocratic grace of the Mughal dynasty, traditional patrons of the arts.*

ABOVE: *The Islamic influence is evident in this ornate window at Old Delhi's Red Fort. The scalloped arch opens the interior to light, while the rhythmic, geometrical patterns provide privacy.*

RIGHT: *A domed turret adds Indian style to a fortress setting, while arches usher welcome breezes into an interior courtyard. The sandy hue of the architecture recalls the golden desert.*

OPPOSITE: *Two stone jalis, or perforated screens, flank a vista from this courtyard into the adjacent garden. Deep blue mosaic tiles evoke images of water and help to create the impression of a lush oasis.*

ABOVE: *These wide, shallow arches are a contemporary interpretation of classic architectural features. The warm spice tint provides a natural-looking backdrop for the varied greens of the courtyard garden, while the crisp white accents lend a cool and gracious note.*

OPPOSITE: *This room boasts a feeling of spacious- ness, thanks to the plethora of arches opening up the area. With their exotic foliated designs, these architectural features elevate ordinary gatherings into celebratory occasions. White key tiles echo the white stuccowork and enhance the light and airy look of the space.*

RIGHT: *An eye-catching arrangement of colorful panes transforms humble wooden doors into a worthy prelude to the grand architecture that lies beyond. Notice how this striking array of colors provides warm contrast to the eggshell hue of the courtyard. Delicate etched patterns appear in both the door panes and the fanlight, offering a delightful surprise as visitors draw close.*

OPPOSITE: *Detailed yet subtle carvings in the wooden doors and the built-in window seat create an overall effect of refined rusticity. Similarly, drapes with radiant gold threads and a bedspread with an elaborate patchwork design lend a luxurious quality to the seemingly straightforward room.*

ABOVE: *The simplest of elements can produce a sense of quiet and introspection. Weight-bearing basket-handle arches add dignity to a humble hallway, while screens in the door and the lancet-arch windows usher in air and light. A cool wash of blue adds to the serenity of the narrow space.*

OPPOSITE and ABOVE: *A contemporary interior manages to incorporate traditional elements while maintaining a fresh appeal. The staggered arrangement of the arches keeps the eye engaged at all levels, while the deep blue used for the backdrop of the display niches creates the illusion of added depth. This riveting hue also appears on the tiled stairs and the painted jali for a unified effect.*

LEFT: *A fretwork arch serves as an airy counterpoint to two solid wood doors. Notice how the decorative arch deftly frames an ornate armoire that holds pride of place in the room beyond, allowing the piece to be enjoyed from both rooms.*

OPPOSITE: *Recalling time-honored jalis, the patterned insets on a door are all it takes to infuse a modern bedroom with an air of tradition. A bamboo blind shades the interior, while lengths of sari silk lend drama to the simple architecture of the window.*

CHAPTER TWO
CAPTIVATING COLORS

India is far too varied to be represented by a single palette. The summer flowers of the Himalayas, the blooms and fruits of the tropics, and the spices that are exported worldwide are all inspirations that can find their tonal equivalents in any home. Nevertheless, color is a ubiquitous, integral part of Indian life, whether appearing in the saris on a Bombay street or the produce stalls of a market in Gujarat. A harmonious riot of color adorns a temple facade in Madurai, a grave Sikh's turban will surprise in fuchsia, and a bouquet of flowers offered at a modest shrine at home will combine yellow and red, the colors of a beloved god.

Because of India's complex cultural heritage, the symbolic values of colors resonate with meanings until they finally resolve into paradoxical purity. For example, green is the color of Islam, but also of one of the manifestations of the Buddhist goddess Tara, in her nurturing aspect. Blue—once the hue that denoted the home of a Brahman, a member of Hinduism's highest caste—is still the color of aristocratic Krishna, an avatar of Vishnu, the sustainer. Not coincidentally, blue is also the hue associated with the life-giving monsoon. To Catholics, it is the color of the Virgin Mary. (On a more practical level, indigo blue is chosen to repel the desert's heat and discourage mosquitoes.)

Vastu Shastra not only guides millions of Indians at home and abroad in the building and orientation of dwellings, but also in color choices. According to some interpretations, Vastu Shastra prohibits the use of strong hues indoors; others recommend colors that embody the kind of energy most appropriate to the room's specific purpose. For instance, the burning reds and warm yellows associated with passion would be optimal selections for a bedroom. Each of the four elements has a corresponding color. Wind (or air) is associated with white or silver; water with blue; earth with clay and terra-cotta; and fire with yellow, orange, and red. The fifth element, space (or sky), has no corresponding color.

OPPOSITE: *Flowers are found everywhere in India—strewn before visiting guests, offered at altars in homes and temples, and lined up or centered on the dinner table for natural adornment. The vibrant hues of the petals shown here can be used to shower a room with radiance or simply to introduce some enlivening accents. Either way, the assertive combination conveys exuberance and energy.*

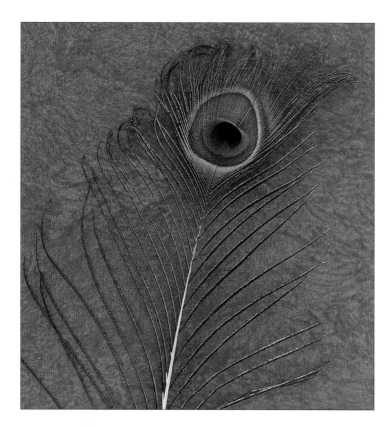

will bring the tropical ebullience of Indian style to an interior. Earth tones and the colors of metals provide an unusual spin on Indian style, whether they appear as one of the many shades of clay or as variations on bronze, copper, gold, or silver.

Color pairings are unexpected and assured. Bright baby blues appear alongside striking pinks, and jewellike greens mix with royal blues as they do in a peacock's feathers. Other combinations take the form of sublimely sophisticated juxtapositions, such as the saffron and plum of Buddhist monks' robes. A similarly powerful contrast is that of mango yellow set against the deep, sober hue of indigo.

Color is a powerful tool that can either bathe a room in Indian drama or simply evoke Indian style through a carefully chosen accent or two. It can work its magic by adorning such architectural features as doorways, windows, moldings, beams, and display niches, as well as by appearing in painted furnishings and textiles. All of these means provide opportunities to explore the manifold sensuous possibilities of Indian color.

As powerful as tradition is in India, personal taste and variations triumph everywhere. Greens range from essential viridian to emerald, lime, and parrot green. Jaipur, in Rajasthan, is known as the Pink City, while Jodhpur, on the edge of the Thar Desert, is the Blue City. The latter delights with its indigo walls, both inside and out. During the last century, synthetic pigments replaced organic indigo and madder in the inexpensive, classic limewash, but the traditional blue and red retain their place in Indian style.

The palette is frequently saturated and bright, and it often affectionately reflects the shades of everyday life. There's the creamy white of the ubiquitous coconut or glossy airaish; the orangish yellows of saffron, mango, and papaya; the elusive, poetic pink-red of rubies; and the deep, lipstick-luscious shades of chili and *kumkum*, the powder women use to create the characteristic dot between their eyebrows. Any one of these hues, whether used on walls or in decorative accents,

ABOVE: *Peacock motifs recur in various incarnations in Indian design, and the bewitching hues of this bird's iridescent plumage are another source of inspiration for interior palettes. A color scheme of greens and blues also recalls the outdoors.*

ABOVE: *The Shivaniwas Palace marries historical architectural elements, such as scalloped arches and a balcony overlooking a regal drawing room, with a bold color combination. Though both the blue and russet are found throughout India, together they form an unexpected alliance.*

ABOVE and OPPOSITE: *A palette of indigo, saffron, and pink infuses this bedroom with Indian ambience. Ancient textile techniques, such as batik, provide a circular pattern in a room where horizontals and verticals subtly dominate. Adding a regal note, flashes of gold appear on the bed and at the window.*

OPPOSITE: *In this audacious living room, indigo blue teams up with a cheerful yellow that infuses the space with the warmth of a tropical locale. The sunny hue offers a flattering backdrop for the sofa, thanks to the powerful contrast between the two. Additional touches of yellow pop up in the toss pillow and in the upholstery of the chairs in the adjacent hallway, where the introduction of aqua brings further drama to the mix. The palette seems to come full circle with the rich dark blue of the steps and the banister, and the yellow covering the wall above the stairs.*

ABOVE: *Perhaps no single color evokes Indian style more than indigo, its very name derived from the region. In this composition of colors and textures, the raw stone of the window remains unpainted, revealing its natural beauty. The textured paint treatment of the wall suggests the soft sheen of airaish.*

ABOVE: *In a dynamic juxtaposition of cool and warm tones, a fiery orange and a night-dark indigo shade one end of a living room. Thanks to their strategic employment, the colors emphasize the geometry of the room, which is defined by walls placed at subtle angles. A graceful sitar becomes a work of art when framed in a display niche. Notice how this niche bears a white backdrop to show off the instrument.*

OPPOSITE: *Yellow, orange, and blue are time-honored Indian hues, appearing here in toned-down shades. The distressed finish of the far wall is in perfect accord with the rustic ceiling beams and large water vessel.*

LEFT: *A modern entertaining area uses neutral hues to great effect, making a splash of bright color a delightful contrast. The hot pink contemporary divan attracts the eye—and encourages leisurely lounging—while travertine marble, wood window frames, and cream-colored walls create an enveloping but low-key sense of warmth.*

ABOVE: *Fun is the dominant note in a playful interior that seems inspired by a child's fantasy of a leopard. On a stone wall, spots lay color upon texture—then leap from wall to table, where they meet a mass of flowers in similar hues. The jumble of colors seems to multiply when reflected by a mirror, which is framed in blue and set against a curry orange expanse of wall.*

ABOVE: *A classic jali shows its colors, spangling a dim interior with brilliantly tinted light. The combination of red and yellow infuses the cool-toned space with warmth.*

RIGHT: *According to Vastu Shastra, white is the color of the element air, but it is also a staple of the daily Indian palette, worn by many, especially in the countryside. Here, a bedroom appears to be softly carved out of creamy white. Wood columns and a few carefully chosen wood accents provide earthy counterpoints to the pale backdrop.*

CHAPTER THREE
FURNISHINGS AND
DECORATIVE ACCENTS

Historically, in India—as in much of the world—social gatherings took place with family, friends, and guests seated on the floor. In a more prosperous home, the floor would be cushioned with layers of fine, pile wool carpets, while bolsters and other pillows made visitors comfortable during long, leisurely evenings conversing and playing *shatranj*, or chess. A man of great wealth or high social status might sit on a *gaddi*, raised slightly higher than his fellows, but for the most part, a symbolic equality predominated, at least among men.

Traditionally, furniture has been limited to a few pieces. One of these is the *bajot*, a typical low table found throughout India, even where European furniture styles otherwise prevail. This piece can be simple and painted or deeply carved in precious wood, such as mahogany or the more classic teak. Pressed into service as a display surface, the bajot provides a handsome resting spot for favorite objects, such as a cherished hammered brass or silver bowl, filled with fragrant petals; a cluster of photographs of loved ones; an inlaid box; or a sentimental souvenir.

In western and central India especially, many rooms, even kitchens, may boast one or more of the formal chest known as a *patara*. Made of ornately decorated leather or metal, the patara holds clothes, prized family possessions, or a bride's dowry.

Another beloved and characteristic piece of furniture found in Indian homes is the *chowkie*, a low stool that is often enhanced with a carved backrest. Undiscriminating, the chowkie appears in all kinds of places, from sophisticated city residences to the courtyards of countryside farms, where variations serve as seats for the demanding task of churning butter.

OPPOSITE: *At the end of a hall, an alcove furnished with a pillow-strewn couch beckons guests onward with the promise of relaxation. A carved wooden screen, originally designed for a window, takes on a new persona above the seating. Not only does it serve as a piece of artwork in its own right, but it also acts as a frame for a collection of shoes.*

ABOVE: *With their tropical associations, caned furnishings bring Indian style into this spacious and hospitable living area. A backless divan invites dozing on lazy afternoons.*

OPPOSITE: *In the adjacent dining room, high beamed ceilings, creamy walls and chair upholstery, and indirect natural light keep everything feeling cool. The bamboo blinds, or chicks, are a classic Indian window treatment.*

The arrival of the Muslims and the spread of the Mughal empire and culture introduced to the baithak the tradition of placing one or more low mattresses against the walls. This arrangement is still found in many Indian homes, as the clean-lined, almost minimalist demeanor lends itself to contemporary design. Today, the mattresses are more often raised slightly—banquette-style. In both its traditional and modern forms, this type of seating gives a room flexibility, allowing it to fulfill several functions. With the addition of a table amidst the long cushions, the area can serve as a relaxing place for conversation, a spot for savoring a soothing cup of tea with friends, or an Indian-style dining room.

Cane and other cool, light woods are used in another time-honored piece of furniture, the more constructed divan. Basically a low couch or daybed, this piece is perfect for napping in the sultry Indian afternoons. In its humbler incarnation, the divan becomes a charpoy—a bed made of string woven on a wood frame. In more modest homes, the lightweight charpoy and bedding are simply leaned against a wall, leaving the central space free for the day's activities.

Wood, whether intricately shaped in traditional designs or simply finished to allow the grain's beauty to predominate, is an essential element of Indian style. This naturally appealing material may appear in the form of a traditional, carved mirror frame for an elegant and practical effect, or it can bring another cultural current into the mix for a personal design masala that nonetheless speaks of harmony.

Perhaps the most characteristic piece of Indian furniture is the swing, which invites aristocratic reclining. In the palace at Jasdan, in Gujarat, a solid silver swing holds pride of place in the maharani's reception room. Grandmother's rocking chair can contribute a similar feeling of movement; in fact, the elaborate carvings, sinuous lines, and affectionately crowded surfaces of Victoriana also have a place in Indian style, providing a subtle counterpoint.

Well-chosen details are enough to bring Indian style into any home. Shining metal accents, such as hammered brass bowls grouped together on a shelf or a large brass vessel that rests on the floor to fill up a corner, bring Indian-style glints to living rooms and bedrooms. Windows dressed in *chicks*, the popular blinds of slender bamboo slats, speak of cool relief from sweltering heat while injecting a room with natural texture. Conveying a similar feeling of comfort, a ceiling fan, slowly revolving, is as evocative as it is practical—a welcoming sight and a symbol of hospitality.

OPPOSITE: *Tradition, ease, and tranquility inform this classic Indian-style interior. A baithak in an arched alcove invites casual conversation—or companionable silences. In the foreground, two long low-slung seats provide additional resting spots.*

ABOVE: *Waiting is no chore in this tiny, impeccably furnished foyer of a Bombay apartment. Cushioned metal chairs flank a small but serviceable cupboard to provide an intimate spot for a tête-à-tête. Directly above the colorful wooden piece, a painted frame enters the mix to form a column of classic Indian details.*

ABOVE, LEFT: *A traditional component of Indian interiors, the swing chair has several names—jhoola, hindola, sankheda, and zhopala—depending upon the part of the country in which it resides. Its connotations touch upon the full scope of Hindu culture, from the social to the spiritual.*

ABOVE, RIGHT: *The chains suspending the swing are as decorative as they are functional—as evidenced by the detail of this figure. Swing ornamentation takes on an infinite number of forms, varying according to function and placement, as well as personal taste. In the northwest, a swing might be brightly decorated with tropical flora and fauna, while elsewhere, bells and tassels might enhance the swing's movement.*

ABOVE: *A simple swing chair with sleek lines and unembellished wood maintains the up-to-date look of this living room while still paying homage to the past. Joined by a pair of banquettes in an L-shape configuration, the swing plays an integral role in creating a comfortable sitting area conducive to conversation.*

OPPOSITE: *A variation on a baithak places plush, pillowed mattresses directly on the floor, where guests can enjoy the cool air that the ceiling fan sends their way. The carpet is Turkish, the bajot virtually universal.*

RIGHT: *Formal decorative trim on a red-painted bookcase gives importance to the tomes within. A fanciful wall treatment conjures up starry Indian nights.*

OPPOSITE: *Bamboo blinds—the ubiquitous chicks—fulfill their practical service while lending a graphic quality to a sparely furnished room. A bajot supports an altarlike assortment of objects, in keeping with the common Indian household practice of regarding the home as a temple.*

ABOVE: *Lavished with pillows, a built-in banquette offers a modern interpretation of traditional baithak seating. The pillows not only provide comfort, but bring an understated mix of patterns to the scene. Delicate bowls in red and blue supply splashes of bold color.*

LEFT: *All over India, verandas and balconies offer shady places to reflect or entertain. The British influence is evident in this long screened porch, where rattan chairs surround tables that seem to be waiting for teatime. The louvered doors temper the harsh rays of the sun, while still allowing in air.*

OPPOSITE: *Surrounding a bajot, the low chairs known as chowkies form an enticing gathering spot. Notice how the painted blue backs of the chairs echo the accents on the floor for a harmonious effect. The setup practically cries out for good food, good drink, and good company.*

ABOVE: *When space is at a premium, a wooden ledge above a doorway provides a wonderful opportunity for displaying treasures collected over the years. Here, the glint of metal immediately catches the eye and draws the gaze upward to a luminous array of traditional brass vessels. Notice how the golden gleam of the metal brings out the soft luster of the wood.*

OPPOSITE: *With its warm embrace, a Tudor arch generously shelters an assemblage of prized Indian objects. At the center of the exotic vignette, red and gold pillows—piled high—take on a sculptural look. The jalis bring additional pattern to the scene, while feathers arranged in a brass bowl contribute soft texture. Beneath the shelf, a patara provides ornamentation as well as storage space. For those who wish to get an up-close look at the delightful collection, a dhurrie rug offers cushioning underfoot.*

ABOVE: *A colorful hanging lantern brings an Indian flair to this eclectic dining area, which also features Victorian Gothic woodwork. Notice how the red accents in the lantern pick up the hue of the patterned banquettes.*

ABOVE: *Perfumed afternoon tea in shining silver patiently awaits company. The massive, well-tended antique table borrows the reflection of red from the carpet, lamp, and pillow—a bold and successful mix of old and new.*

ABOVE: *With its low, floor-hugging profile, an innovative arrangement recalls the pairing of a traditional bajot with baithak seating. Yellow cushions provide comfort on the wooden framework and, along with a ceramic vase of cheerful blooms, brighten up the area. Other uplifting touches of yellow appear on the mullions and drapes in the background. When the French doors are open, occupants reap the benefits of fresh air and experience the sensation of lounging outside.*

OPPOSITE: *The antique and the contemporary make good neighbors in this Indian-style hallway. A flight of floating wood steps allows light to shine on a heavy sideboard, which in turn plays host to a collection of favorite objects. On the wall, ornate shutters with delicate blue detailing bring life to the white backdrop, while a vase below chimes in with additional color.*

OPPOSITE: *A metal-frame bed—painted white, covered in white linens, and cloaked by a sheer white canopy—promises a peaceful night's sleep. Touches of color, introduced by the hanging artwork and the cloth draped over the bedside table, have been carefully chosen so as not to interfere with the tranquility of the space.*

ABOVE: *The unmistakable courtly elegance of Mughal painting casts its glamorous spell over any interior. Miniatures in the Persian style are typical of the sophisticated arts that flourished under the emperors of this bellicose dynasty.*

ABOVE: *Wood and textiles define this room's decor. The tenting overhead seems to be anchored at the windows—an illusion that is achieved by using valances made out of a similarly patterned fabric. Flanking the bed, brass-trimmed night tables, in a popular export style, contribute a stately note that is worthy of the majestic bed. Accents of madder red provide warm finishing touches.*

LEFT, TOP: *With its elaborate carvings, a wooden table reveals the beauty of Indian craftsmanship. Swirling floral designs provide a softening counterpoint to the straight lines and angles of the octagonal surface, thereby resulting in a soothing balance. So that the delicate workmanship of the table may best be appreciated, decorative objects are limited to a pair of brass elephants, which shine against the dark wood.*

LEFT, BOTTOM: *A jumble of textures is responsible for the powerful appeal of this charming vignette. Printed white muslin, decorated with timeless motifs, meets a cowrie shell–edged, quilted textile in hot spice colors. Bougainvillea, the emblematic flower of the tropics, stands in a metal vase, neighboring a brass statuette. A diminutive pot, in a shape unchanged for millennia, holds incense.*

LEFT, TOP: *In a traditional Indian home, favorite possessions live out in the open. Elaborately chased and lovingly polished silver, mirrored in a table's gleaming surface, adds its own light to a bright interior.*

LEFT, BOTTOM: *At the heart of Indian design lies an appreciation of the senses. Here, mesmerizing flames attract the eye, offering a peaceful spot on which to focus. Floating petals contribute color and texture while suffusing the air with their sweet fragrance.*

ABOVE: *An ornate vessel adorns a corner of a formal Indian home, transforming empty space into an area that merits attention. Thanks to its similar hue, the decorative container functions as an effective bridge between the wood door frames, creating a smooth transition.*

CHAPTER FOUR
PRECIOUS TEXTURES

India's fabrics, from Madras cotton to cashmere wool, are well known in households throughout the world. In ancient times, Greeks, Arabs, and Egyptians admired and wore prized Indian cotton. Calico, the printed cotton that traveled westward across North America with the pioneers, takes its name from Calicut, today Kozhikode, a lively port in southwest India. In the 1960s and early 1970s, attractive, affordable prints arrived in North American college dorm rooms, on the wave of a popular culture suddenly enriched by Indian style. Today, the rich hues of pashmina shawls accent a multitude of clothing styles, while colorful sari silks flutter poetically in front of apartment windows.

Of all the handicrafts for which India is famous, none are more varied than the country's textiles. Coir mats—woven into timeless patterns—offer natural texture, while homespun cottons printed with synthetic pigments speak of the incredible beauty that lies in simplicity. On the more lavish end of the spectrum, priceless silks exude regality with their deep jewel tones wrung from traditional vegetable dyes, and lush carpets handmade from inimitable Ladakhi wool imbue surfaces with a sense of luxury. Velvet, which is often enhanced with mirrorwork—thought to repel the evil eye—or shot with gold or silver embroidery, adds an extravagant touch.

Whether employed throughout a room or sprinkled here and there as powerful accents, Indian-style textiles lend a sensuous quality to any setting. The choice of textures, colors, and patterns is virtually infinite, ranging from the abstract designs of paisley, born of the Islamic prohibition against any literal representation of the world, to elaborate printed or tie-dyed designs, some thousands of years old, some boldly contemporary.

During the sixteenth century, the Mughal emperors encouraged the manufacture of carpets, hand-knotted of wool or silk, often with cotton to strengthen the weave. The classic dhurrie, made of cotton or sometimes wool, usually features geometric patterns. Strategically placed, carpets add elegance to a sparsely furnished space, while swathes hanging on walls offer a refined and refreshing alternative to framed artwork.

OPPOSITE: *Texture is pattern in the third dimension. Here, dappled light falls on richly embroidered fabrics, creating an atmosphere that is at once luxurious and meditative. The gold mullions through which the sunlight enters enhance the majesty of the mix.*

A living room or den transforms into a traditional baithak with the addition of carpets and cushions of all shapes and sizes. But it takes only a single evocative accent to give a room an Indian flavor. Draped casually yet artfully over the back of a sofa, a length of sari silk will inject a resounding Indian note into a living space. Similarly, a shimmering sari-inspired curtain hanging seductively in a window will introduce an exotic touch that enchants and delights. Heavier, fringed textiles will bring a sense of distinction to an ordinary table, while a pair of toss pillows covered with mirrorwork will jazz up a bland banquette.

In the bedroom, textiles find manifold applications. Canopies and other bed curtains may be made of the sheerest muslin or heavy, opulent velvets; fine-mesh mosquito netting adds a tropical, romantic, and practical touch. Mix and match fabrics and patterns to achieve a personal interpretation of Indian ambience. For all-out drama, draped walls and ceilings create the sensation of a royal hunting tent.

Textiles are only part of the equation. The balance between lively pattern and serene space that is characteristic of Indian style is galvanized when these deceptively simple fabrics are combined with other textures. These additional components may appear in the form of other textiles, carved woods, incised or river-smooth metals, or tilework and pottery. As in the cuisine of India, which harmoniously combines cultural ingredients from the world over, yet leaves room for each cook's masala, Indian style requires some knowledge, a lot of imagination, and a talent for knowing when to break the rules.

LEFT: *Embroidery over a heavy woven textile makes for an opulent accent. This is particularly true when the background is a traditional chili red and the geometric needlework designs are executed in gold, thereby creating an unmistakably subcontinental effect.*

OPPOSITE: *An array of textiles brings comfort to a sitting area. Gracing the floor, a heavily patterned carpet enlivens the dark wood of the bajot above it. Embroidered pillows line up along both the couch and the divan, ready to provide cushioning for those who wish to sit back and relax. On one wall, a striking swathe of fabric provides a softening touch and makes for a dynamic accent.*

LEFT, TOP: *Silk saris from Kanchipuram are some of the most opulent textiles in all of India. So much precious metal is woven into the finest of these that they are sold according to the weight of the gold and silver in them.*

LEFT, BOTTOM: *A bold red paired with turquoise blue provides powerful contrast in this sari from Kanchipuram; luminous gold embroidery heightens the drama. Saris such as this exemplify the Indian gift for mixing patterns and colors. Capable of transforming a room, these stunning textiles can be employed as wall hangings, curtains, or sofa throws for an incomparable impact.*

OPPOSITE: *Printed cotton designs mix effusively against the patterns of a mosaic floor. The use of blue and white ties the scene together, creating a cool impression of ordered profusion and sensual comfort.*

OPPOSITE: *Sheer cloud-white silk billows in the slightest puff of a breeze—a sail on a ship of dreams. The caned divan below displays an array of textiles—woven, embroidered, and quilted—all of which can be shifted and rearranged for individual comfort.*

ABOVE: *A closer look at one of the pillows reveals the extraordinary amount of detail that goes into adorning textiles. Hand-embroidery, as in this ancient pattern, is as precious as jewelry; it adds dimension to any fabric surface and depth to any decor. It can also contribute contrasting hues or, as here, enhance an overall color scheme.*

ABOVE: *Rustic wood shutters stand in contrast to a filmy length of lemon yellow fabric glittering with gold accents. Textiles make it easy to change the look and feel of any room when the whim strikes.*

OPPOSITE: *The makings of an Indian-style dining area can be exported anywhere. In this garden room, a layered treatment of textiles brings a taste of India to the table. Displaying a deft use of color, the arrangement features a simple, orange-yellow tablecloth peeking out beneath a piece of fuchsia fabric adorned with festive gold embroidery. The gold accents echo the hue of the underlying cloth, tying the two components together. The surrounding flowers and foliage make any other form of decoration unnecessary.*

OPPOSITE: *Indian style with a light hand: in a Madras apartment, pillows provide classic and contemporary accents, while the prevalence of wood refers back to traditional architecture. A chowkie backs against a stepped room divider.*

RIGHT: *Indian style is so rich, its traditions so varied, that it lends itself to infinite interpretations. Here, muted yellows, oranges, and reds arranged in modern variations recall the look of ancient Indian patterns.*

BELOW: *Traditionally hung over a doorway, a toran finds new life as a valance at a window. In its current role, the colorful length of fabric not only provides a bit of shade, but also bestows an air of importance upon the objects resting below.*

OPPOSITE: *Employed strategically, textiles can produce an architectural effect. In this nurturing bedroom, fabric falls in soft columns and drapes for an intimate, informal canopy. The wall color acts as a heartening backdrop, emphasizing a personal masala of patterns. Light filtering through a wicker chair reveals the piece's airy texture, which is counterbalanced by a sturdy wooden chest of drawers.*

ABOVE: *A carved and painted plaster chair recalls the inventive creations of the people of the Thar Desert, near Jaisalmer, in the northwest. The contoured chair becomes more inviting with the addition of plump cushions. Decked out in red and gold hues, these comforting accents feature distinct patterns on either side for variety.*

OPPOSITE and BELOW: *This suite may have been inspired by a* dal-badal, *a regal tent from the Jodhpur area. All is texture: a furled chick acts as an informal lintel, mutlicolored fringe demarcates wall and ceiling, and heavy woven cotton carpets offer softness underfoot. Overhead, the design on the tented ceiling creates the impression of the sun shining down upon the inhabitants.*

ABOVE: *Filtered natural light floods the bathroom, where an antique tub contradicts the impromptu accent of a folding wooden camp stool. Hardwood floors and yards of fabric create another playful contrast, between temporary and permanent.*

ABOVE: *This room is a successfully orchestrated symphony of textures, from the brass bajot to the softly shining terrazzo floor to the raw masonry arches above the leaded windows. The red and gold pillows make regal accents for the patterned purple cover. All the different decorative elements come together to produce an effect that is positively radiant.*

OPPOSITE: *Texture, textiles, and color are confidently combined in a deft alchemy of ancient and modern. Below a timeless beamed ceiling, a classic mix of indigo and curry yellow is lightened with a sheer canopy of pale lavender. In an inverted twist on reality, the floor is bedecked with a smattering of stars, as well as a moon. The latter echoes the curve of the wall—a detail that speaks volumes about how closely all the elements in the room work together.*

PHOTO CREDITS

Courtesy of Anna French,
Ltd.: 89

©Dinodia Picture Agency:
58 left, 58 right, 64, 66, 72,
76 top, 77

Elizabeth Whiting &
Associates: ©Jon
Bouchier: 69; ©Andreas
v. Einsiedel: 87, 90
bottom; ©David Giles:
86; ©Lu Jeffery: 32, 44;
©Di Lewis: 49, 68, 70;
©Mark Luscombe-White:
5, 7, 8, 16, 21 right,
26–27, 29, 34, 35, 38, 40,
47, 50, 52, 63, 65, 73, 74,
75 bottom, 76 bottom, 78,
84, 85, 92, 93 top, 93

bottom, 94, 95; ©Mark
Nicholson: 45; ©Spike
Powell: 91; ©Mark
Thomas: 2, 37, 42, 43

FPG International:
©Michael Goodman: 26

©Anne Gordon Images:
20, 21 left, 22, 25 top

Houses & Interiors:
©Verne: 36, 60, 71;
©Simon Butcher: 50–51, 61

Interior Archive: ©Tim
Beddow: 14, 30, 31, 33,
54 (Owner: Moore), 55
(Owner: Moore), 56;
©Ianthe Ruthven: 28
(Designer: Anokhi), 81;
©Fritz von der Shulenburg:
41, 67 (Designer: Anokhi),
83 (Designer: Anokhi),
90 top (Designer: Anokhi)

©B. S. Kumar: 46
(Architect: Rohit Shinkre),
48–49 (Architect: Kiran
Kapadia), 57 (Architect: S.
Rajshekhar), 59 (Architect:
Kiran Kapadia), 88
(Architect: Rohit Shinkre)

Leo de Wys, Inc.: ©Picture
Finders: 11

©David Sanger
Photography: 19

©Elliot Smith: 82 top, 82
bottom

©Tim Street-Porter: 12, 15

Trip Photo: ©J. Hurst: 23,
80; ©H. Rogers: 75 top

©Dominique Vorillon: 62

©Jessie Walker: 24, 25
bottom